GUTSY DAREDEVILS

BY VIRGINIA LOH-HAGAN

45TH PARALLEL PRESS

Published in the United States of America by Cherry Lake Publishing Group
Ann Arbor, Michigan
www.cherrylakepublishing.com

Reading Adviser: Beth Walker Gambro, MS Ed., Reading Consultant, Yorkville, IL
Book Designer: Melinda Millward

Photo Credits: Cover: © Zach/Adobe Stock; Page 1: © Zach/Adobe Stock; Page 5: © Yusnizam Yusof/Shutterstock; Page 6: © Anant Kasetsinsombut/Shutterstock, © Cathy Keifer/Dreamstime; Page 7: © Zach/Adobe Stock; Page 8: © Cathy Keifer/Shutterstock; Page 10: © Zuzana Lovasova/Shutterstock, © nattanan726/Shutterstock; Page 11: © Pefcon/Shutterstock; Page 12: © Barbara Ash/Shutterstock, © Sergey Uryadnikov/Shutterstock; Page 13: © Matej Hudovernik/Shutterstock; Page 14: © Kjersti Joergensen/Shutterstock; Page 16: © Janelle Lugge/Shutterstock, © Polbkt/Shutterstock; Page 17: © Polbkt/Shutterstock; Page 18: © wrangel/iStockphoto, © Anton Jankovoy/Shutterstock; Page 19: © Arun Sankaragal/Shutterstock; Page 20: © Arun Sankaragal/Shutterstock; Page 22: © David & Micha Sheldon/Thinkstock, © Luis Louro/Shutterstock; Page 23: © Hivaka/Shutterstock

Graphic Element Credits: Cover, multiple interior pages: © paprika/Shutterstock, © Silhouette Lover/Shutterstock, © Daria Rosen/Shutterstock, © Wi_Stock/Shutterstock

Library of Congress Cataloging-in-Publication Data

Names: Loh-Hagan, Virginia, author.
Title: Gutsy Daredevils / written by Virginia Loh-Hagan.
Description: Ann Arbor, Michigan : Cherry Lake Publishing, [2023] | Series: Wild Wicked Wonderful Express. | Audience: Grades 2-3 | Summary: "Who are the gutsy daredevils of the animal kingdom? This book explores the wild, wicked, and wonderful world of daring animals. Series is developed to aid struggling and reluctant young readers with engaging high-interest content, considerate text, and clear visuals. Includes table of contents, glossary with simplified pronunciations, index, sidebars, and author biographies"—Provided by publisher.
Identifiers: LCCN 2022042725 | ISBN 9781668920763 (paperback) | ISBN 9781668919743 (hardcover) | ISBN 9781668922095 (ebook) | ISBN 9781668923429 (pdf)
Subjects: LCSH: Animal locomotion—Juvenile literature. | Animals—Adaptation—Juvenile literature.
Classification: LCC QP301 .L678 2023 | DDC 591.5/7—dc23/eng/20220916
LC record available at https://lccn.loc.gov/2022042725

Cherry Lake Publishing Group would like to acknowledge the work of the Partnership for 21st Century Learning, a Network of Battelle for Kids. Please visit http://www.battelleforkids.org/networks/p21 for more information.

Printed in the United States of America
Corporate Graphics

About the Author
Dr. Virginia Loh-Hagan is an author, university professor, former classroom teacher, and curriculum designer. She is not a daredevil. She likes being safe and sound in her home. She lives in San Diego with her very tall husband and very naughty dogs.

Table of Contents

Introduction

Animals do daring things. They make big jumps. They climb walls. They go fast.

They risk their lives. They don't do it for fun. They do it to **survive**. Survive means to stay alive. They live in the wild. They have to be smart. They have to be brave. They use their skills.

Some animals are **daredevils**. Daredevils are wild. They do dangerous things. Some animals are more daring than others. These animals are the most exciting daredevils in the animal world!

Orangutans take risks. Seven out of 10 adult orangutans break arms or legs.

Geckos

Geckos climb walls. These lizards climb steep cliffs. They hang upside down. They dare to climb anything.

Geckos have sticky toes. They cling to surfaces. They quickly run up. They stick and unstick their feet. They do this 15 times a second.

Unlike other climbing animals, geckos just use their toes to climb.

There is *one* surface geckos can't stick to! It's the nonstick coating found on cookware.

Gecko feet have more than 500,000 tiny hairs per foot. These hairs have split ends. The tiny hairs bond with the surface. Each hair grips the surface. All the hairs together create a tight hold. This is how geckos stick to things. They have super climbing powers.

When Animals Attack!

Paul Rosolie dared a green anaconda to eat him. Anacondas are one of the largest snakes in the world. They eat large animals such as jaguars, deer, and pigs. They squeeze **prey** to death. Prey are animals that are hunted for food. Rosolie found a 20-foot-long (6 meter) anaconda. He was in South America. Rosolie **provoked** it. To provoke means to anger. The anaconda pounced. It wrapped itself around Rosolie's body. Rosolie wore a helmet. The anaconda clamped its jaws on his helmet. Rosolie felt his arm breaking. He asked his team to rescue him. The team got him out.

Sloths

Sloths live in jungles in Central and South America. They dare to spend their lives upside down. They hang by their claws. They have special claws. Their claws are long and curved. They have strong grips. They don't fall. They even stay hanging after death!

Their bodies are made for hanging. Their organs are fixed in place. They can't walk upright on the ground.

Sloths have long tongues. Their tongues stick out 12 inches (30 centimeters). They can turn their heads almost all the way around.

Sloths have hair that grows from their bellies to their backs.

Orangutans

Orangutans are strong. These apes are 7 times stronger than humans. They live in the Southeast Asian islands. They live in tall trees. They build nests. They're the largest animals to live in trees. Adult males can weigh as much as 300 pounds (136 kilograms)!

Orangutans dare to swing through these trees. They have no safety nets. They don't worry about falling. They swing to eat. They swing to avoid danger on the ground. Their bodies are made to swing. Their feet are like hands. They can grip easily.

Female orangutans carry their babies through the trees.

Orangutan moms will stay close to their babies for up to 9 years!

Orangutans are very smart. They use tools. They use leaves as umbrellas. They use leaves as toilet paper. They use branches to scratch their backs.

Humans
Do What?!?

Humans do daring things for fun instead of for survival. They push limits. Alexander Rusinov is called the Russian Spider-Man. He climbs walls. He jumps between rooftops. He does handstands on the edge of skyscrapers and bridges. He hangs from tall buildings. He dangles from hundreds of feet in the air. He doesn't use safety wires.

Tree Snakes

Asian tree snakes move through Asian rainforests. They have an extreme way of moving. They dare to climb without arms and legs.

They climb steep surfaces. They climb tall trees. They have scales on their bellies. They use their bellies to climb. They fly across treetops. Their bellies act like a **parachute**. A parachute is a safety device. It looks like the top of a balloon. The snakes' bellies catch the air. The snakes get pushed forward. This helps them glide from tree to tree. They don't land. They crash. Their bellies flop against the tree. This doesn't seem to hurt the snake.

Tree snakes fall from high places.

Bharals

Bharals are mountain sheep. They live 14,000 feet (4,267 meters) above ground. They live in the Himalayan Mountains in Asia. These are the highest mountains in the world.

Bharals are daring climbers. They have **flexible hooves**. Flexible means they can move easily. Hooves are the hard part that covers the feet of some animals. Bharal hooves grip the rocks. Bharals climb steep mountains. They balance on mountain cliffs.

Bharal hooves help them grip the rocks on steep cliff faces.

Bharal lambs are born in late June and July.

Bharals take great risks. Only half survive their first year. But bharals are safer on the cliffs than on the ground. **Predators** can eat them on the ground. Predators are hunters.

Did You Know...?

- Inventors created climbing tools. They studied sticky forces. They were inspired by gecko feet.

- Sloths digest food slowly. They only need to use the bathroom once a week!

- Flying snakes are better gliders than flying squirrels.

- Arctic foxes wait for baby barnacle geese to fall. They eat the dead or injured babies.

Baby Barnacle Geese

Barnacle geese live in the Arctic. They nest at the top of high cliffs. They nest about 300 feet (91 meters) above ground. They're far away from predators. They're also far away from food.

Baby barnacle geese can't fly. They can barely walk. But at 1-2 days old, they are like daring **BASE jumpers**. BASE jumpers jump off objects from high places.

To leave the nest, the baby barnacle geese step off the cliff. They fall into the water. They can't fly. They have a 90 percent chance of surviving the fall.

Baby barnacle geese free-fall from a cliff.

Consider This!

Take a Position! Some animals are built to be daredevils. Humans have to invent tools to help them be daredevils. What are some examples of this? Do you think humans should be daredevils? Why or why not?

Think About It! Some animals are in danger of losing their homes. For example, humans are destroying rainforests. This affects several animals in this book. What do you think about this issue?

Learn More
- **Article:** National Geographic Kids - "Orangutan." March 1, 2014: https://kids.nationalgeographic.com/animals/mammals/facts/orangutan.
- **Article:** National Geographic – "These Snakes Can Jump—and Scientists Want to Know Why" by Jason Bittel. November 14, 2019: https://www.nationalgeographic.com/animals/article/jumping-flying-snakes-australia-evolution

Glossary

BASE jumpers (BAYS JUHM-purs) people who jump off objects from high places

daredevils (DEHR-deh-vuhls) people or animals who do dangerous things

flexible (FLEK-suh-buhl) easy to move

hooves (HOOVZ) the hard part that covers the foot of an animal such as a sheep or horse

parachute (PAR-uh-shoot) safety device that helps people glide or fall

predators (PREH-duh-turz) animals that hunt other animals for food

prey (PRAY) animals hunted for food

provoked (pruh-VOHKD) angered someone or something

survive (sur-VYV) stay alive

Index